CRICKET WORLD CUP

GLOBAL CITIZENS: SPORTS

Published in the United States of America by Cherry Lake Publishing
Ann Arbor, Michigan
www.cherrylakepublishing.com

Content Adviser: Liv Williams, Editor, www.iLivExtreme.com
Reading Adviser: Marla Conn, MS, Ed., Literacy specialist, Read-Ability, Inc.

Photo Credits: ©coopder1/iStock, cover, 1; ©benoitb/iStock, 5; ©Patrick Eagar/Patrick Eagar Collection/Getty
Images, 6; ©Mitch Gunn/Shutterstock, 7, 8, 11, 13, 18, 20, 25; ©Harris & Ewing/Library of Congress/ Reproduction
No. 2016890733, 12; ©Arif Ali/AFP/Getty Images, 14; ©Lance Bellers/Shutterstock, 17; ©Mitch Gunn/Dreamstime, 19;
©Mitchell Gunn/Dreamstime, 21, 22; ©Colin Edwards/Alamy Stock Photo, 27

Library of Congress Cataloging-in-Publication Data

Names: Hellebuyck, Adam, author. | Deimel, Laura, author.
Title: Cricket World Cup / written by Adam Hellebuyck and Laura Deimel.
Description: Ann Arbor, Michigan : Cherry Lake Publishing, [2019] | Series: Global Citizens: Sports |
    Audience: Grades 4 to 6 | Includes webography. | Includes bibliographical references and index.
Identifiers: LCCN 2019004153 | ISBN 9781534147492 (hardcover) | ISBN 9781534150355 (paperback) |
    ISBN 9781534148925 (pdf) | ISBN 9781534151789 (hosted ebook)
Subjects: LCSH: World Cup (Cricket)—History—Juvenile literature. | World Cup (Cricket)—Juvenile literature.
Classification: LCC GV923 .H45 2019 | DDC 796.358—dc23
LC record available at https://lccn.loc.gov/2019004153

Cherry Lake Publishing would like to acknowledge the work of the Partnership for 21st Century Learning.
Please visit *www.p21.org* for more information.

Printed in the United States of America
Corporate Graphics

ABOUT THE AUTHORS

Laura Deimel is a fourth grade teacher and Adam Hellebuyck is a high school social studies
teacher at University Liggett School in Grosse Pointe Woods, Michigan. They have worked
together for the past 8 years and are thrilled they could combine two of their passions, reading
and sports, into this work.

TABLE OF CONTENTS

CHAPTER 1

History: World Cup: Past and Present

Cricket is a popular sport in schools and clubs all over the world. The International Cricket Council, the group that organizes cricket matches between countries, has 105 members. Each of these countries competes for a chance to enter the Cricket World Cup tournament every 4 years. But how did this sport begin?

The Beginning of Cricket

Cricket most likely began during **medieval** Europe as a game between two players. However, no one is quite sure of the real **origin** of the sport. Many believe that it started as a child's game. There is evidence that cricket was played at a school in Surrey,

Where did the name *cricket* come from? Some people say it comes from the medieval French word *criquet*, which is a type of stick.

England, as early as 1550. The new game quickly gained popularity throughout England. School teams organized into clubs where players would meet, set rules, and play games regularly. The most famous club is the Marylebone Cricket Club in London, England. It established the rules for cricket around the world in 1788. The Marylebone Cricket Club still sets the rules for cricket today, even for the Cricket World Cup!

The first Women's Cricket World Cup was held in 1973.

Playing the Game

In the beginning, cricket was simple. It was like baseball. The game had a pitcher and a batter. Except in cricket, the pitcher is called a bowler and the batter is called a batsman. The bowler would toss a ball like object, like a rock, to the batsman, who would then attempt to hit it. Over time, the game became more complex. Instead of just hitting the ball to score a point, the batsman would hit the ball and run to a set location to score points. A batsman who struck the ball to a certain area could score runs without having to actually run!

Since a cricket match can last many hours, the games
begin very early in the morning.

There are two parts to a cricket bat: the handle and the blade.

The game also added a **wicket**. Wickets are made up of small sticks, called bails, and stumps. The batsman needed to protect the wicket from being hit with the ball. As more rules were added, the game started to get longer and longer.

The Start of the World Cup

Despite the complex rules, cricket quickly became popular around the world. The first international game was played between Canada and the United States in 1844. Canada defeated the

United States by 23 runs. At the time, there were international cricket games being played, but there was no tournament to decide a world champion. Cricket was added as an event at the 1900 Summer Olympics, but afterward, cricket was removed as an Olympic sport.

Cricket fans attempted another tournament in 1912 with the Triangular Tournament in England. However, due to poor public interest, it was a one-time event. Fast-forward to the 1975 Prudential World Cup in England. Eight teams participated in this historic event: Australia, England, India, New Zealand, Pakistan, the West Indies, Sri Lanka, and East Africa. Because of the success and popularity, the tournament was hosted every 4 years after that.

Developing Questions

The average Cricket World Cup game lasts over 8 hours! This time includes the game's two innings (where the team gets to bat) and the required "tea break" where players can rest. Why do you think cricket matches are so long? Do you think this needs to be changed? Why or why not?

CHAPTER 2

Geography: Cricket Worldwide

The 2019 Cricket World Cup featured 10 different countries. Some of these countries, like India, have been in the tournament since it began in 1975. Other countries started to compete in the World Cup far later. For instance, Afghanistan became the 20th team to qualify for the tournament in 2015. All of these countries have unique stories of their experiences with both cricket and the World Cup.

People who play cricket are called cricketers. There are 11 players on each side, with a "12th man" available to play if a cricketer gets hurt during a game.

England and Wales

Both England and Wales cohosted the World Cup in 2019. This was the fifth time that both countries have hosted! There were 48 different matches between the 10 countries that competed. Many of these matches were in famous stadiums. The first match was held at The Oval in London, England. The Oval has hosted cricket matches since it opened in 1845. The final cricket match was held at Lord's Cricket Ground, also in London. This arena has held cricket matches for over 200 years!

The first bat and ball game to be played in the United States wasn't baseball, but wicket, a game closely related to cricket.

India

Cricket is very popular in India. Although the country does not have an official national sport, many Indians claim that if the country did, it would be cricket. It's no surprise they believe this, as there are over 54 million people who participate in the sport. That is more people than the population of Kenya or Spain!

India has cohosted the Cricket World Cup three times since the World Cup began. However, for the first time, India will host the World Cup in 2023 on its own.

Because of South Africa's racial policies, the country was banned from playing international cricket from 1970 to 1991.

Shaoib Akhtar of Pakistan is said to be the fastest bowler in cricket. During the 2013 World Cup, he bowled the ball at 100.2 miles (161.3 kilometers) per hour!

West Indies

Cricket is also popular in the West Indies. The West Indies is a region around the Caribbean Sea, south of Florida and north of South America. This region is made up of many different islands. The team from the West Indies has been very successful in World Cup tournaments. The team won the first two tournaments in 1975 and 1979 and made the finals in 1983.

The West Indies hosted the World Cup in 2007. Matches were held on seven different islands in the Caribbean: Barbados, Jamaica, Saint Lucia, Trinidad, Antigua, Grenada, and Saint Kitts. Matches were also held in Guyana, a country in South America.

Gathering and Evaluating Sources

While cricket is a popular game around the world, it is most popular in the following countries:

India	*Pakistan*
Bangladesh	*Sri Lanka*
Afghanistan	*Nepal*
Jamaica	*Australia*
Trinidad and Tobago	*New Zealand*
Barbados	*England*

Using the resources at your library and on the internet, research why cricket is popular in these countries. What do these countries have in common?

CHAPTER 3

Civics: Playing the Game

Since cricket started in medieval Europe, the game's rules have evolved. There are many different ways to play cricket, with Twenty20, Test, and One Day being the most popular. These are different from each other by the number of overs (pitches) allowed for each batsman and how long the game can take. The World Cup follows One Day cricket rules.

Winning the Game

There are several ways to score points in cricket. One way is to hit the ball past the boundary of the outfield. If the ball flies past the boundary in the air, the team earns six points. If the ball bounces and then goes past the boundary, the team earns four points.

There are 11 players on a team.

"Bowled out" in cricket means that the bowler knocks down the opposing team's wicket during a bowl.

Cricketers can also earn points through runs. There are two batsmen on the field at a time. One is "on strike," meaning the person who the bowler pitches to. Pitches in cricket are referred to as bowls. The other is at the opposite end of the field ready to run. When a batsman hits the ball, he can run to the other side of the pitch and trade places with his teammate. If the two batsmen trade places before the ball is thrown back to the wicket, they score a run.

If batsmen use any part of their body to protect the wicket from a bowled ball, they might be dismissed. This is called "leg before wicket" (LBW).

If in a single innings a batsman scores 100 or more runs,
it is called a "century."

In cricket, the word *innings* is used to describe both one inning and more than one!

It is common for teams to have very high-scoring matches. For example, in 2003 Australia defeated India by 125 runs to win the World Cup.

Innings

In a World Cup cricket match, each team gets to bat once. This is called an innings. All 11 players on a cricket team get to bat during an innings. In the Cricket World Cup, a batsman gets to bat until he or she is out, or has been bowled to 50 times! A single innings can last many hours during the Cricket World Cup.

The 2021 Women's Cricket World Cup will be held in New Zealand.
This will be the third time the country has hosted the Women's World Cup.

Qualifying for the Tournament

Ten countries **qualified** for the 2019 World Cup. (In the 2011 and 2015 World Cup, there were 14 countries that qualified.) The host country always qualifies for the tournament, so both England and Wales automatically got spots. Seven other teams also automatically qualify for the World Cup. These are the top seven cricket teams in the world. This is decided by the number of matches a team wins and the number of points they score in matches. If there were remaining spots in the World Cup, it would be decided by a separate tournament.

Developing Claims and Using Evidence

Think of a game you like to play. What are the rules of this game? Why do you think these rules were written for the game? Are there rules you would like to add or change? Now think about the game of cricket. There are rules that were drafted as early as the mid-1700s. Since then, the rules of cricket have been rewritten six times. If you had the chance to rewrite a few rules in the Cricket World Cup, what would you change? Why? Use evidence you find from your library and the internet to support your reasoning.

CHAPTER 4

Economics: It Pays to Play

Players who compete for a World Cup championship are often paid very well by their teams. Players earn money in a number of different ways when they play cricket. The amount of money cricketers earn is different based on who they play for.

Paying for Cricket Play

Players on national cricket teams have a large **variance** in how much they make. Each player on a cricket team has a **contract**. Each player gets a different contract from the team based on his or her ability and skill level. In addition to this contract, players earn money for every match they play in.

Virat Kohli of India is said to be the highest-earning cricketer to date.
Most of the money he makes comes from sponsors!

Taking Informed Action

Think about what you have read about the players and the **discrepancies** *between team contracts and their* **endorsements**. *Then, read the chart below with more information on how much money cricketers make from different countries.*

Player	National Team	Total Amount Made in 2017
Virat Kohli	India	$26.9 million
MS Dhoni	India	$19.7 million
Chris Gayle	West Indies	$7.5 million
AB de Villiers	South Africa	$5.5 million
David Warner	Australia	$5.5 million
Steven Smith	Australia	$2.5 million

Besides their ability to play cricket, what are some other reasons why players might make such different amounts of money? Do you think this is fair? Why or why not? Share your thoughts with a relative, teacher, or friend. How do you think this could be changed?

Australian international women players will earn an average of about $148,000 by 2021. This is a huge increase from 2017 when they were earning only $56,000 on average!

The team with the highest-paid players in the world is India. The top contract for an Indian player in 2018 was $311,775. The lowest contract for Indian players was $75,000. The team with the lowest-paid players in the world is Zimbabwe. The top contract for a Zimbabwean cricket player in 2018 was $100,000. This was for the captain, Graeme Cremer. The average contract for the rest of the team was around $55,000.

Endorsements

In addition to getting paid to play the game, cricketers also make money through endorsements. Cricketers receive money from many different businesses and groups to endorse their products—even groups not connected to the game.

Cricket players can earn a lot of money through endorsements by doing something very simple: putting a sticker on their bat. A player can put a sticker of a business logo on their bat, which fans will see when that player is batting. The player does not have to do anything else to earn money from these bat endorsements. Virat Kohli, the captain of the Indian national team, has the largest endorsement from a company today. The Madras Rubber Factory, India's largest tire producer, paid him 1 trillion Indian rupees ($13,905,000) over 8 years to have its sticker on his bat!

Communicating Conclusions

Cricketers endorse many different products for businesses. For example, the highest-paid cricketer in India, Virat Kohli, endorses many different products. Take a look at some of the products he endorses below:

Brand	Type of Product
Puma	Athletic wear
MuveAcoustics	Electronics
Too Yumm	Healthy snacks
Tissot	Watches
American Tourister	Luggage
Boost Energy Drink	Energy drinks
Uber India	Ride-sharing

In interviews with reporters, Virat Kohli says he only endorses products he believes in. Think about the items in the chart above, then think about your own life. What types of products would you endorse? Would you ever agree to endorse a product you did not believe in? Why or why not? Share your ideas with a relative, friend, or teacher.

Think About It

There are many different ways to score points during a cricket match at the World Cup. There are also many ways for a player to get out in cricket. Take a look at some of the ways a batsman can be out in a World Cup cricket match:

- Bowled: The bowler knocks the bails from the stumps on the wicket before the batsman can hit the ball.

- Caught: A player in the field catches the ball before it hits the ground.

- Hit the ball twice: A batsman hits the ball twice with his or her body or the bat.

- Hit wicket: A batsman hits the wicket when swinging.

- Obstructing the field: A batsman gets in the way of the fielders when running to the opposite side of the bowl.

- Retired: A batsman stops batting and leaves the pitch when it's his or her turn, without the referee and opposing team captain's permission.

Using your local library and the internet, look at other ways that cricketers get out in a match. Then, think about games you like to play with others. Could you add any of these rules to the games you like to play? How might you change them to fit your game? Can you think of any others?

For More Information

Further Reading

Gifford, Clive. *ICC Cricket World Cup 2019 Kids' Handbook.* London: Carlton Books, 2019.

Kerr, Jim. *How to Improve at Cricket.* Tunbridge Wells: Ticktock Media, 2008.

Websites

ICC Cricket World Cup: England and Wales 2019
https://www.icc-cricket.com/cricket-world-cup
This is the official website of the Cricket World Cup, with information on the tournament's rules, upcoming matches, and other news.

International Cricket Council—What Is Cricket?
https://www.icc-cricket.com/video/298515
The video at this site explains how cricket is played.

GLOSSARY

contract (KAHN-trakt) an agreement to work for a certain amount of money

discrepancies (dis-KREP-uhn-seez) things that are different from each other

endorsements (en-DORS-muhnts) giving your support or approval for an item or activity

medieval (mee-DEE-vuhl) during the time after the fall of the Roman Empire and before the Renaissance

origin (OR-ih-jin) the point or place something begins or is created

qualified (KWAH-luh-fyed) to be allowed to do something

variance (VAIR-ee-uhns) difference

wicket (WIK-it) a set of three stumps that a bowler must hit in order to get a batter out in cricket

INDEX

[21ST CENTURY SKILLS LIBRARY]